1
Belfry or Halles Tower, a unique Flemish building 13th- 15th century.

Market Square.

Statue of Jan Breydel and Pieter de Coninck — popular heroes and freedom-fighters (1302-1304), erected in their honour in 1887. In the background, the 19th century Provincial Court.
A number of other historic buildings can be seen on the Market Square. A house with a 15th century gable on the corner of the St. Amandstraat is topped with a compasscard. Opposite stands «Craenenburg» House where Archduke Maximilian of Austria was held prisoner in 1488 when the populace rebelled against his government. Several houses on the Market Square used to belong to the guilds, and some of them still display the symbol of their history in their architecture: the gable of the weavers' guild house is crowned with a basket, and the date 1621 shows when work began on the fishermen's guild house.

2

Victory Bell.

On the 220th step of the Belfry or Halles Tower, the visitor can glimpse the famous «Victory Bell», with a diameter of 2.05 m. This bell is only rung on very exceptional occasions.

3

Carrilloneur at the keyboard.

Although the tones produced by the belfry's automatic mechanism are a pleasure to the ear, they cannot tank in purity of sound and tone with the music played on the keyboard.

4 *Post office —*
Market Square

5 *Market Square, Belfry*
and Pronvincial Court.

6
*The Burg —
the Law
Court — the
Town
Clerk's
Office —
Town Hall.*

8
*Basilica of
the Holy
Blood.*

7
*Town Hall
— the
Gothic
Room.*

9

Saint Basil's Chapel (the Crypt).

This chapel, or Crypt, was built in the 12th century by Diederik van den Elzas, Count of Flanders. The Saint Basil's Chapel or Crypt has kept its original form and is the only Romanesque building of its kind in West Flanders.

10   11

In this chapel is preserved the beautiful 14th century masterpiece of Our Lady of Charity, also known as the Pietà. The Ecce Homo statue can aslo be seen here: a great work of art and an unrivalled piece of wood-carving.

12

Basilica of the Holy Blood (interior).

13

Shrine of the Holy Blood.

14

According to tradition the relic of the Holy Blood was brought to Brugge at the time of the Second Crusade, having been venerated in Constantinople. Every year in May, on Ascension Day, the Procession of the Holy Blood files through the decorated streets of the town. The shrine of the Holy Blood is unquestionably the most valuable treasure preserved in the museum of the Chapel of the Holy Blood: it is made of gold and silver encrusted with precious stones, the work of Jan Crabbe (17th century).

Old Recorders House.

16

*An excursion through Brugge in a horse-drawn coach has
its charms.
Through the «Blinde Ezelstraat», under the archway called
the «Bridge of sighs».*

17

The Green Quay.

The Green Quay at night.

The Green Quay with (far right) «De Pelikaan» almshouse (17th century).

20
Rozenhoedkaai and
Belfry — top right:
17th century Tanners'
House
(Huidevettershuis).

21
Wollestraat with
Belfry and (right) old
patrician house.

22
Groeninge Museum,
«Philip the Good» —
Rogier Van der
Weyden (copy)
Photographic archive,
Groeninge Museum,
Photographer M.
Platteeuw, Brugge.

23

Groeninge Museum
"The Virgin with the Canon Joris van der Paele" Jan Van
Eyck (+ 1441).
Photographic archive, Groeninge Museum.
Photographer: M. Platteeuw, Brugge.

Groeninge Museum
"The Last Judgment" Hiëronymus Bosch (+ 1516).
Photographic archive, Groeninge Museum.
Photographer: M. Platteeuw, Brugge.

25
*Surroun-
dings of the
Gruuthuse
Museum and
the Church
of Our Lady.*

26

Inner courtyard of the Gruuthuse Museum with (upper right) part of the adjacent 12th century Church of Our Lady.

27

Gruuthuse Museum — mounted statue of Louis of Gruuthuse.

Gruuthuse Museum. General view of the kitchen.

The Gruuthuse palace.

The palace now serves as a museum, where a most varied patrimony is on exhibition: lace, coins, tapestries, musical instruments, weapons, furniture, kitchen equipment and so on. There is also a stone museum with tombstones and archaeological findings on display.
The entire group of buildings is dominated by the spire of Our Lady's Church, which ranks in majesty with the tower of the Belfry.

29
Garden of the Arentshouse — Bridge of St. Boniface.

30
Old wooden gable, near the Bonifacius Bridge behind the Church of Our Lady.

31
*Main altar
and organ.*

32
*The
mausoleum
of Maria of
Burgundy
(1495-1502).*

The Church of Our Lady. The aisles of this temple are embellished to this day with countless treasures. In paintings alone she is one of the richest churches in Brugge. Among the famous signatures collected here in the museum are those of Gerard David, Isenbrant, Van Eyck and others. Maria of Burgundy and her father Charles the Bold are buried in the Church of Our Lady.

33

"Madonna and Child" (1503-1504) White marble statuette.
Michelangelo.

Saint John's Hospital with on the right the entrance of the Memling Museum.

35
A magnificent arch in which the death and coronation of the Virgin are represented.

*Saint John's Hospital
part of the oldest buildings.*

In one of the old wards, a number of Jan Memling's finest works are on view. The jewel of the collection is "The Mystical Marriage of Saint Catherine" 38 "Sybilla Sambetha" 37 "Martin Van Nieuwenhove", the "Pièta", "The Adoration of the Magi" and the "Saint Ursula Shrine" have also enraptured countless visitors.

Memling, who was of German origin, after spending periods in Cologne and Brussels, settled definitively in Brugge, where he became a Free Master of Saint Luke's Guild in 1467. A rather more poetic though not altogether verifiable account of his life tells how he was wounded at the Battle of Nancy while serving Charles the Bold as a mercenary soldier. According to this legend, he bequeathed a number of his masterpieces to the Saint John's Hospital in recognition of the good treatment he received there.

39
Walplaats with spire of Church of Our Lady.

The Lace Centre
In former times the art of lacemaking was practised by
many women in Brugge; the skilled tradition was handed
down from mother to child.
Modern progress has to some extent blighted the deft
fingercraft of bobbins and stitches.
The lace school in Brugge was started in order to keep up
the ancient tradition; here the fine art of bobbin
lacemaking is taught to young and old.

40
Lacemakers of Brugge.

41
Lacework.

42

Bridge and entrance to the Princely Beguinage «Ten Wijngaarde».

The buildings of the old Beguinage, situated at the water's edge, date back to the 13th century. The Beguinage developed with the entry into it of girls from all social backgrounds who devoted themselves to a mystical community life, under the guidance of a superintendent called the Grand Mistress.
The Beguinage is undoubtedly the most peaceful spot in Brugge. Nowadays the same Beguinage is still open to those who choose to withdraw for a quiet retreat from our intensely active society, to find peace through devotion and prayer.

*Princely Beguinage «Ten Wijngaarde».
The Chapter-House.*

*Another pleasant sight along the canals and their green
banks are the swans of Brugge. Their decorative forms
unconsciously reflect the attractiveness of the town.*

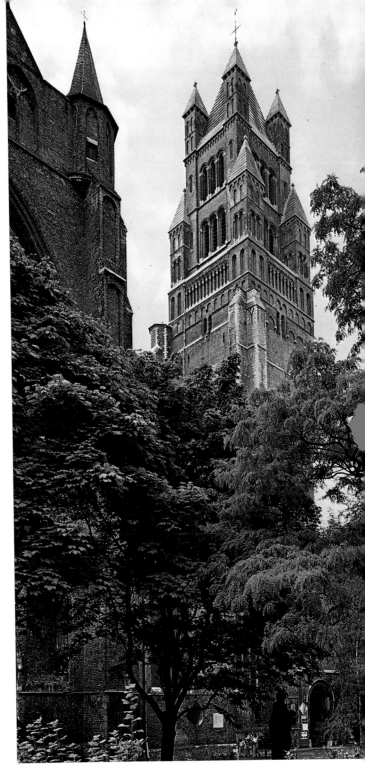

*Princely Beguinage «Ten Wijngaarde». Entrance seen
from inside.*

*Tower of Saint Saviour's Cathedral (12th to 13th
century).*

*Saint Saviour's Cathedral is in fact much older; it was
built in the 9th century and has on more than one
occasion been the victim of fire. This sanctuary was
raised to the stature of a cathedral in 1834, and prides
itself on being the oldest brick building in Belgium.*

*It contains numerous treasures, bequeathed and endowed during its long history, or forming an integral part of the
whole, such as: the sculpture of the Creator by A. Quellin (1682); the main choir, decorated with the coat-of-arms of
the Knights of the Golden Fleece; the magnificent stained-glass windows; richly woven tapestries and monumental
tombs which testify to its glorious past. A valuable collection of paintings by Flemish masters can be seen in the Saint
Saviour's Cathedral museum; these works are all perfect of their kind, and seem to have been painted by angelic
hands.*

*Saint
Saviour's
Cathedral.
Early 18th
century
bronze door
under the
organ loft.*

*Saint
Saviour's
Cathedral.
Choir.*

49
The "Ezelpoort".

50
The "Kruispoort" (15th century) with historical museum.